DOABLE TEMPEST

William Shakespeare's Comedy In "Do Able" Form

by

Brent Nautic Von Horn

DOABLE TEMPEST

Copyright © 2020 Brent N. Von Horn

All rights reserved. Printed in the United States of America. No part of this book may be used or reproduced in any manner whatsoever without written permission except in the case of brief quotations embodied in critical articles or reviews.

This work may be performed before live audiences, provided a license to do so is obtained from Brent N. Von Horn prior to performance. See detailed information on how to obtain such license at the back of this book, or contact the author at:

Nautic Publishing

Brent N. Von Horn

https://www.nauticproductions.com

Cover design by Nautic Productions © 2020 Brent N. Von Horn

Cover art by John Williams Waterhouse (1849-1917)
oil painting titled "Miranda"

ISBN: 978-1-7349239-8-8 (Paperback); 978-1-7349239-9-5 (eBook)

First Edition, 2020

10 9 8 7 6 5 4 3 2 1

CONTENTS:

Introduction	i
Synopsis	iii
Characters	v
PROLOGUE	1
ACT 1	2
ACT 2	31
ACT 3	51
ACT 4	70
ACT 5	84
EPILOGUE	101
Character Notes	103
Set Design Notes	114
Production License	117

Introduction

William Shakespeare is often revered as the Greatest Playwright ever. However, he lived 400 years ago and in modern times actors and audiences both have trouble understanding him. These "Do Able" versions of Shakespeare's plays are true versions of his works, still mostly using the Bard's words, but edited to be more easily comprehensible.

Believe it or not, there are some who say there was no such person as William Shakespeare, that he was made up as the pseudonym of some other writer. There is little in the historical record to document the life of William Shakespeare. It could be possible that some educated member of high society wrote under the name of "William Shakespeare" to avoid the scandal of being associated with theatre. His plays were written in the years when bubonic plague epidemics ravaged London, and theatres were dirty places. The "players" who acted were all men, by law, as the stage was not considered suitable for women. Whoever Shakespeare was, he wrote for the audiences of his time. He wrote for the low-browed, uneducated, illiterate masses, who wanted action, sex, bawdy insults and scandalous subject matter. In the same plays, he also wrote for the high-brow elite, the educated and cultured top tier of his society, who appreciated poetry, love and tales of honor.

The goals of this Do Able version remain the same, aiming at the right balance of both fun and art, as that balance has changed over the years since Shakespeare's time. For actors, plotlines are explained, character breakdowns are provided, and stage directions (not written down in Shakespeare's time) are provided. For audiences, the original text is adapted, to make it more palatable to modern ears, while still retaining the magic and beauty of Shakespeare's writing. This means, largely, the cutting of some minor characters, as well as many lines of dialogue where (measured by our short-attention-span culture) Shakespeare perhaps waxed a bit too poetic and strayed away from his plotlines and action. Some scenes are entirely rewritten.

Yet, enough remains to be true to the original. If we've succeeded in writing this book, you will need nothing else in order to perform an outstanding production of William Shakespeare's *The Tempest* with more clarity and effect than ever before.

Synopsis

Twelve years before, Prospero, the Duke of Milan, and his daughter, Miranda, were driven out of power by Prospero's own brother, Antonio. They were set to drift at sea, there to die. Fortunately, one of Prospero's friends, Gonzalo, managed to load their boat with food, clothes, and Prospero's prized collection of spell books.

Prospero and Miranda made their home on an uncharted island, where Prospero studied his books and became a strong magician. With his dark arts he learned to control spirits. And he was finally able to see his chance for revenge.

The King of Naples and some of his lords, including Antonio, sailed past Prospero's island on their way to celebrate the marriage of the King's daughter. As their fleet was on its return voyage home, Prospero caused a tempest to wreck the King's ship and dump its passengers on his island's shores. There, he directed the spirits to make the survivors' lives miserable.

The King's son, Ferdinand, lands alone, believing all others to have drowned. By putting him in contact with his daughter, Prospero soon sees their love blossom, and they decide to wed.

The King mourns for the son he believes drowned. Prospero intervenes to stop an assassination plot against the King, but then causes them to go mad.

Only once Ferdinand and Miranda have declared their love, does Prospero relent and allow the King and his men to return to sanity. Prospero reveals himself then to them, and forgives their past actions. The King returns Prospero's dukedom to him.

As a last instruction for the spirits, Prospero has them return the King's ship and crew, unharmed. Prospero then releases the spirits to be free, and destroys his magic books.

Characters

Prospero	the former Duke of Milan
Ariel	a spirit servant to Prospero
Miranda	Prospero's daughter
Caliban	slave to Prospero
Ferdinand	Prince of Naples
King Alonso	King of Naples
Antonio	Duke of Milan (Prospero's brother)
Sebastian	King Alonso's brother
Gonzalo	King Alonso's counsellor
Trinculo	King Alonso's steward
Stephano	King Alonso's butler
Captain	]
First Mate	]
Mariners	] crew of the King's ship
Spirits	spirits who take on multiple roles, including the roles of Iris, Ceres and Juno in Prospero's play, and act as hellhounds

THE TEMPEST

by William Shakespeare

PROLOGUE

Enter Prospero, above.

PROSPERO
Twelve long years have I waited for this singular opportunity which now opens before me.
Revenge most sweet, for the longer delayed.
What has been taken from me must be taken back, now that I myself have power to move the elements.

(He raises his staff. Ariel and Spirits enter, dancing wildly. Strong winds begin to howl.)

With power comes freedom, fear and redemption.
Freedom and redemption for me! And for others, cold hard fear.

(Lightning flashes, with thunderous booms.)

It is time! Let fear rule this night!

(Prospero exits.)

ACT 1

SCENE 1

Ariel climbs into the rigging of a ship, in the midst of a terrifying storm. Spirits caper around the ship.

The ship's crew struggle to survive.

CAPTAIN
First mate!

FIRST MATE
Here, Captain! What cheer?

CAPTAIN
Speak to the crew! Fire them up to give their best, or we run ourselves aground.

FIRST MATE
Where are we, Captain? Surely there's no land on our charts nearby.

CAPTAIN
That's just it. This sudden squall has blown us

far too near to an island I've some odd
recollection of. A rocky crag not on our charts.
Go to, sir! Lest we all perish, mariner and noble
passengers alike.

> *(Captain climbs to look out into the darkness with his telescope.)*

FIRST MATE
Hey, me hearties! Cheerly, cheerly, me hearts!
Take in the topsail! Pull, pull for your lives, pull
and give nothing back! Holdfast the jib, hold
there, or we shall all find our ship's company
splashed upon the sharp and deadly rocks!

> *(Enter King Alonso, Sebastian, Antonio, Ferdinand, and Gonzalo.)*

KING ALONSO
Good Mate, have care. Where is the Captain? Is
there nothing to be done about this tossing?

FIRST MATE
Good King, I pray now, keep below.

ANTONIO
Where is the Captain? He must level out our
course!

Act 1 Scene 1

FIRST MATE
Sir! You mar our labor. Get your king and noble men below, and keep your cabins. You do but assist the storm up here in our way!

ANTONIO
It is the king's desire to be on deck. Nay, be patient.

FIRST MATE
When the sea is!

(Ariel dumps a bucket of water on their heads.)

KING ALONSO
This weather is exhilarating!

FERDINAND
Father! In weather like this, might we be looking for mermaids and sea nymphs?

FIRST MATE
(to Gonzalo)
You are the king's counsellor. Can you not persuade him to quit the deck?

GONZALO
(to King Alonso)
My lord, perhaps 'twould be best to retire.

KING ALONSO
My son wishes to see a mermaid!

(A Spirit jumps into the rigging, bringing another bucket of water to Ariel. They laugh and he dumps the water on King Alonso.)

KING ALONSO
Yes, Counsellor, I see your point. Come!

(The Noblemen exit.)

FIRST MATE
Lay her ahold, ahold! Set her two courses, off to sea again! Lay her off!

CAPTAIN
(jumping down)
We're against the lee shore!

(Ariel bangs a gong.)

MARINERS
We're on the rocks! Mercy on us! We will split! We will split!

(More Spirits climb into the rigging, dumping buckets of water onto the men.)

Act 1 Scene 1

FIRST MATE
Captain, we'll need a sea anchor!

CAPTAIN
'Tis too late, Mr. Phelps. Make what peace you can with your maker.

(Antonio and Gonzalo return from below.)

ANTONIO
Captain, captain! You've sprung a leak below!

CAPTAIN
It's no drier up here, sir!

MARINERS
We split! Have mercy on us, God above! We sink!

ANTONIO
Let's all sink with the king.

(He exits.)

FIRST MATE
Me thinks he may succeed at that!

(Ariel and the Spirits laugh. They all bang on Ariel's gong.

Ferdinand enters.)

FERDINAND
(to Gonzalo)
They turn green below!

GONZALO
(to Ferdinand)
Now would I give a thousand ships for one acre of dry land. The wills above be done, but I would fain die a dry death.

(Gonzalo exits.)

FERDINAND
What?! Look, mermaids! No, storm nymphs! I am sure I saw faces, but for a second! These waves are full of devils!

(Ariel and Spirits bang their gong repeatedly.)

MARINERS
Rocks! We're on the rocks! She'll break and dump us all!

(All but Ariel and his Spirits exit.)

ARIEL
So breaketh apart the ship
and into the briny depths its men,

as did my master bid.
Come, Spirits! We still have work to do!

(Ariel and the Spirits dance around, playfully mopping up water and pushing towels around, before they exit.)

SCENE 2

On the island, before Prospero's home. The storm still blows.

Prospero and Miranda enter.

MIRANDA
Is it your art, dear father, that has
put the wild waters in this roar?
Oh, I have suffered with those that I saw suffer!
A brave vessel, who had, no doubt, some noble
creatures in her, I saw atop the waves one
moment, and then gone the next!

(Prospero looks out and smiles. He lifts his arms, and the storm dies down.)

PROSPERO
Collect yourself. Be now no more amazed. Tell

your piteous heart there's no harm done.

MIRANDA
Oh, woe! I cannot look away, hoping to catch
but one more sight of that doomed ship.

PROSPERO
No harm, I tell you.
I have done nothing but in care of thee,
of thee, my dear one, thee, my daughter, who art
ignorant of what thou art, or who your father
was once.

MIRANDA
Ignorant, only because you've refused to tell me.

PROSPERO
'Tis time I should inform you further. Lend thy
hand and pluck my magic garment from me.

(She helps remove his cloak, and lays it down where he points.)

Lie it down there, the robe of my art. And wipe
thine eyes, my daughter. I have with such
provision in my art so safely ordered that there
is no soul lost tonight. Sit down, for thou must
now know who you are.

MIRANDA
You have often begun to tell me what I

am, but stopped and left me hanging, as you'd
conclude, "Stay. Not yet. You're not of age."

PROSPERO
The hour's now come.
Obey, and be attentive. Can you remember
a time before we came to live in this hut?
I do not think you can, for then you were not
past three years old.

MIRANDA
Certainly, sir, I can.

PROSPERO
Can you? Of any other house or person?

MIRANDA
'Tis far off, and rather like a dream. Had I
not four or five women once that tended me?

PROSPERO
That's so and more, Miranda. But how is it
that this lives in thy mind? What seest thou else
of how we came to live here on this island?

MIRANDA
But that I do not.

PROSPERO
Twelve year since, Miranda. Twelve years since
thy father was the Duke of Milan and
a prince of bureaucratic power.

MIRANDA
Sir, are not you my father?

PROSPERO
Thy mother was a piece of virtue, and
she said you were my daughter. And your father
was Duke of Milan. And his only heir
was a young princess.

MIRANDA
Oh, the heavens!

PROSPERO
By foul play were we heaved here.

MIRANDA
Please, speak farther.

PROSPERO
My brother and your uncle, called Antonio –
I pray thee, mark me – that a brother should
be so perfidious! – he whom next to thee
of all the world I loved, and to him gave
the manage of my state, as I the liberal arts
studied.
The government I cast upon my brother,
and to my state became a stranger. Your uncle –
do you attend me?

*(Miranda looks back from
gazing out at the sea.)*

MIRANDA
Sir, most heedfully.

PROSPERO
Antonio it was that changed my creatures,
or else new formed 'em, to see him and not me
as Duke of Milan. – Thou attend'st not.

> *(Miranda again is caught gazing out at the sea.)*

MIRANDA
Oh, good sir, I do.

PROSPERO
I pray thee, mark me.
I, thus neglecting worldly ends, was dedicated
to closeness and the bettering of my mind.
My library was dukedom large enough.
But by being so retired, an evil nature
awaked in my false brother. He began
to believe that he himself should Duke be!

MIRANDA
Could my grandmother have begot such an
uncle? Good wombs have borne bad sons.

PROSPERO
Antonio did court the King of Naples,
King Alonso, being an enemy of mine.
Together, they plotted. The king conferred

fair Milan, with all its honors, upon my brother.
Whereon, one midnight, a treacherous army
me and thy crying self hurried thence from
town.

MIRANDA

Alack, for pity!
I, not rememb'ring how I cried then,
will cry it o'er again.

PROSPERO

Hear a little farther,
and then I'll bring thee to the present business
which now 's upon us, without the which this
story were most impertinent.

MIRANDA

Why did they not kill us?

PROSPERO

Aye, my tale provokes that question. Dear, they
durst not, for fear how may react the people of
Milan.
Instead, they took us far to sea on a bark, and
then set us adrift to die in a boat without sail or
mast.

MIRANDA

Oh, what trouble was I then to you!

PROSPERO

Oh, a cherubim thou wast, and it was you that
did preserve me.

MIRANDA
How came we ashore?

PROSPERO
By providence divine.
My brother Antonio sent us out,
under the care of his friend, Gonzalo,
who 'twas, too, a friend of mine, thankfully.
Gonzalo broke his orders and provided us
with food and water, and clothing, what
furniture you see, and blessedly, my books.

MIRANDA
Gonzalo. Would that I might
but ever see that man, and give thanks.

PROSPERO
Sit still and hear the last of our sea-sorrow.
Here in this island we landed, and here
have I, your schoolmaster, educated you more
than other princes true.

MIRANDA
And heavens thank you for't. But father,
I pray you finish your tale to present; tell me
your reason for raising this sea storm last night?

PROSPERO
By accident most strange, bountiful Fortune hath
brought mine enemies sailing near. But here,
cease your questions. Thou art inclined to sleep.

(Miranda falls suddenly asleep.)

Come now, servant, out of the shadows.
Approach, my Ariel. Come.

(Enter Ariel, with a couple Spirits flitting nearby.)

ARIEL
All hail, great master!

PROSPERO
Hast thou, spirit, performed to point the tempest
that I bade thee?

ARIEL
To every article.
I boarded the King's ship; now on the beak,
now in the waist, the deck, every cabin.
I stirred amazement and drove the mortals to
think they were escaping, even as did they steer
their ship direct upon the rocks.

PROSPERO
My brave spirit!

ARIEL
I caused such consternation, all but mariners
plunged in foaming brine and quit the vessel.
Thunder deafened! The King's son, Ferdinand,

with eyes like goose eggs and knees shaking,
was the first man that leaped. He cried, "Hell
is empty and all the devils are here!"

PROSPERO
Ha, ha! But was this nigh ashore?

ARIEL
Close by, my master.

PROSPERO
But are they, Ariel, safe?

ARIEL
Not a hair perished.
On their ennobled garments, not a blemish,
but fresher than before; and, as thou bad'st at me,
in troops I have dispersed them 'bout the isle.

PROSPERO
Of the King's ship, of the mariners? Say
how thou hast disposed of the rest of the fleet.

ARIEL
Safely in harbor is the King's ship, with
her mariners, whom I have left deep asleep in
her hold. As for the rest of the fleet,
which I dispersed, they have all met again
and are upon the Mediterranean float,
bound sadly home for Naples,
supposing that they saw the King's ship

wrecked.

PROSPERO
Ah, Ariel, thy charge exactly is performed.
But we have more work to do.

ARIEL
Is there more toil? Surely, I have performed
sufficiently to warrant my freedom, now!

PROSPERO
How now? Moody? Dost thou forget
from what a torment I freed thee?

ARIEL
No.

PROSPERO
Thou dost. Thou forgets how much you owe me.

ARIEL
I do not forget, sir.

PROSPERO
Thou liest, malignant thing. Hast thou forgot
the foul witch Sycorax, who for her heinous
crimes was banished with her son, Caliban,
to this very island?

ARIEL
Ah, Sycorax!

PROSPERO
Must I remind you every month how she captured you and imprisoned you inside a pine tree for twelve years of torturous confinement?

ARIEL
No! Say not her name again!

PROSPERO
Remember then, how much you owe me, and let's hear no more from you of wanting your freedom.

ARIEL
I thank thee, master.

PROSPERO
If thou again murmur'st, I will rend an oak and peg thee in its knotty entrails till thou has howled away another twelve winters.

ARIEL
Pardon, master!
I will be correspondent to command and do my spiriting gently.

PROSPERO
Do so, and do it well, just as I instruct you, and after two days I will discharge thee.

ARIEL
That's my noble master!

What shall I do? Say, what? What shall I do?

PROSPERO
Go make thyself like a nymph o' the sea. Be
subject to no sight but thine and mine, invisible
to every eyeball else. Go, hence, with diligence!

(Ariel and spirits exit.)

Awake, dear heart, awake. Thou hast slept well.

(Miranda wakes.)

MIRANDA
The strangeness of your story put
heaviness in me.

PROSPERO
Shake it off. Come on,
we'll visit Caliban, my slave, who never
yields us kind answer.

MIRANDA
'Tis a villain, father.

PROSPERO
But rough as he is, he does make our fire,
fetch in our wood, and serves in offices
that profit us. – What ho, slave, Caliban!
Thou villain, thou, speak!

CALIBAN (O.S.)
There's wood enough already.

PROSPERO
Come forth, I say. There's other business for thee.
Come, thou tortoise.

(Enter Ariel, like a water nymph.)

Fine apparition! My quaint Ariel,
hark in thine ear.

(He whispers to Ariel.)

ARIEL
My lord, it shall be done.

(Ariel exits.)

PROSPERO
Thou poisonous slave, come forth!

(Enter Caliban.)

CALIBAN
As wicked dew as e'er my mother brushed
with raven feather from unwholesome fen
drop on you both.

PROSPERO
For this, be sure, tonight thou shalt have cramps,

and when you roll over, the downside will itch
uncontrollably.

CALIBAN
Oh, you cruel interloper. When will you leave?
This island's mine, by Sycorax, my mother,
which you took from me. When thou cam'st first,
you stroked me and gave me water with berries in't,
and taught me to name the big light and the less
that burn by day and night. And then I loved thee.
And showed thee all the qualities of this isle,
the fresh springs, brine pits, fields barren and
fertile. Cursed be I that did so!

PROSPERO
Thou most lying slave,
whom stripes may move, not kindness,
I have used thee, filth, with humane care,
and lodged thee in mine own cell, till thou didst
seek to violate the honor of my child.

CALIBAN
Oh, ho, oh, ho! Would 't had been done!
Hadst thou not prevented me, I had else
peopled this isle with little Calibans.

MIRANDA
Abhorrèd brute, to think I pitied you.
Took pains to make you speak, taught you
one thing or another.

Act 1 Scene 2

CALIBAN
You taught me language, and my profit on't
is I know how to curse.

PROSPERO
Hagseed, hence!
Fetch us in fuel, and be quick, or I'll
rack thee with cold cramps and fill thy bones
with aches, to make thee roar like beasts.

CALIBAN
No, pray thee.
(aside)
I must obey. His art is of such power, I
have no defense against him.

PROSPERO
So, slave, go hence.

(Caliban exits.)

MIRANDA
(aside)
Though he is hideous, still he is the
only male on this island, father apart, and
mayhap my best chance lies in little Calibans.

*(Enter Ferdinand, and
invisible Ariel, playing and
singing.)*

ARIEL

Come unto these yellow sands,
And wipe your hands.
Curtsy when you have, and kiss
The air you miss.
Foot it neatly here and there,
Then turn round and your ass bare.
Hark, hark!

> *(The Spirits bark like dogs.)*

The watchdogs bark.

> *(The Spirits bark like dogs.)*

Hark, hark!

FERDINAND

Where does this music come from? Oh,
it sounds no more. I'm sure, it waits upon
some god o' the island. It lured me on,
and followed it I have, but then stopped.
No, it begins again.

ARIEL

Full fathom five thy father lies.
Of his bones are coral made.
Those are pearls that were his eyes.
Nothing of him that doth fade
But doth suffer a sea change
Into something rich and strange.
Sea nymphs hourly ring his knell.

> *(Spirits ring bells.)*

Hark, now I hear them: ding dong bell.

FERDINAND
This ditty does recall my drowned father, and
where before was fun, now I find sadness.
This is no mortal business.

PROSPERO
(to Miranda)
The fringèd curtains of thine eye advance
and say what thou seest yond.

(Miranda suddenly sees Ferdinand.)

MIRANDA
What is it, a spirit?
Lord, how it looks about! Believe me, sir,
it carries a brave and handsome form. But it is a
spirit, too wondrous to be real.

PROSPERO
No, wench, it eats and sleeps and hath such senses,
as we have, such. This gallant which thou seest
was in the wreck. You might'st call him
a goodly person. He hath lost his fellows
and strays about to find 'em.

MIRANDA
I might call him
a thing divine, for nothing natural
I ever saw so noble.

PROSPERO
(aside)
It goes on, I see, as my soul prompts it.
(to Ariel)
Spirit, fine spirit, I'll free thee
within two days for this.

(Ferdinand sees Miranda.)

FERDINAND
Oh! Most sure, the goddess
on whom this mystical music attends!

MIRANDA
I hear only the natural wind, sir.

FERDINAND
No doubt, the natural state of beauty
for you, accompanying you every day.
If I may only know – oh, you wonder! –
Are you a maid or no?

MIRANDA
No wonder, sir. But certainly, a maid.

FERDINAND
You speak my language! Heavens!
I am the best of them that speak this speech.

PROSPERO
(coming forward)
The best? What wert thou if the King of Naples

heard thee?

FERDINAND
A single thing, as I am now, that wonders to
hear you on this far and barren island
speak of Naples. The King does hear me, and
that he does I weep. Myself am Naples. I am
king, now.
With mine own eyes, I beheld King Alonso, my
father, wrecked and thrown into the angry sea.

MIRANDA
Alack, for mercy!

FERDINAND
Yes, and more! Swimming with him in the
depths are all his lords, and the Duke of Milan.
Somehow, I, King Alonso's son and prince,
alone made it safely to shore, prince no more.

PROSPERO
(aside)
Why already have they eyes only for each other.
(to Ferdinand)
A word, good sir. I fear you have
done yourself some wrong. A word.

MIRANDA
(aside)
Why speaks my father so ungently? This
is the third man that e'er I saw, the first
that e'er I sighed for. Oh, let not my father

find some fault with this noble!

FERDINAND
(to Miranda)

Oh, if a virgin,
and your affection not gone forth to another, of course,
and should'st thou be willing to let it go forth, of course,
I'll make you Queen of Naples.

PROSPERO
Soft, sir, one word more.
(aside)
They are both in either's powers, as if I am not
even here. But this swift business
I must uneasy make, lest too light winning make
the prize light.
(to Ferdinand, finally getting his attention)
One word more; I charge thee,
that thou attend me. Thou dost here usurp
the name thou own'st not, and hast put thyself
upon this island as a spy, to win it
from me, the lord on 't.

FERDINAND
No, as I am a man!

MIRANDA
There's nothing ill can dwell in such a temple.

PROSPERO
(to Ferdinand)
Follow me.
(to Miranda)
Speak not you for him. He is an imposter.
(to Ferdinand)
Come. I'll manacle thy neck and feet together.
You are my prisoner.

FERDINAND
No. Never, sir. You are not even armed!

(He draws his sword.)

MIRANDA
Oh, dear father, please do not hurt him!

PROSPERO
Hence! Hang not on my garments!

MIRANDA
He just got here! Please let me play with him!

FERDINAND
Dear maid, fear not, for this old man has naught
with which to put me at risk – Ack!
Heavens! I cannot move!

(Prospero taps lightly with his staff and knocks Ferdinand's sword out of this hands.)

PROSPERO
Come, boy. There is a fitting place to lock you up.

FERDINAND
Go I will, for now my feet work again.
I go willingly, for if in this prison there is space
enough from which to behold this maid, I ask
no more.

PROSPERO
(aside)
It works.
(to Ferdinand)
Go, that way.

MIRANDA
(to Ferdinand)
Be of comfort. My father's of a better nature,
sir, than he appears just now. I think he likes
you!

(Ferdinand and Miranda exit.)

PROSPERO
(to Ariel)
Thou shalt be as free as mountain winds,
but only if you exactly do
all points of my command.

Act 1 Scene 2

ARIEL
To the syllable.

(All exit.)

ACT 2

SCENE 1

Another part of the island.

Enter Gonzalo.

GONZALO
This way, 'tis drier and the land higher!

Enter Prospero, above.

PROSPERO
Foul men, hated adversaries, look at them now.
They come ashore lost, as I once was. Let them
feel the pain of losing everything!

*(Lightning and thunder
causes Gonzalo to dive down.*

Prospero exits.

*Enter King Alonso,
Sebastian, and Antonio.)*

GONZALO
(to King Alonzo)

I beseech you, sir, be merry. You have cause –
so have we all – of joy, for our escape
is much beyond our loss. Our hint of woe
is common; every day some sailor's wife,
the masters of some merchant, and the merchant
have just our theme of woe. But for the miracle –
I mean our preservation – few in millions
can speak like us.

KING ALONSO

Prithee, peace. No more. I've told you already,
be quiet.

SEBASTIAN
(aside to Antonio)

He receives comfort like cold porridge.

ANTONIO
(aside to Sebastian)

Gonzalo talks but to hear himself. What's
here in this forlorn place to talk about?
This "miracle" has left us on a rock,
to die in bits, 'stead of quickly and blissfully
undersea.
What thinks thou? Will he, for a good wager,
defy his King and crow again?

SEBASTIAN

Against my brother's stern admonition to keep
his yammering mouth shut?

ANTONIO
Look at him work his jaw. To be silent kills the man.

SEBASTIAN
And yet, he speaks not. I'll take that wager. What do we wager?

ANTONIO
A laugh.

SEBASTIAN
'Tis a match.

GONZALO
Though this island seems to be desert –

ANTONIO
Ha, ha, ha!

SEBASTIAN
So. You're paid.

GONZALO
Uninhabitable and almost inaccessible –

SEBASTIAN
He winds up. Could he have something to say?

GONZALO
The air breathes upon us here most sweetly.

How green the grass looks! And our garments,
though drenched in the sea, what ho!
Methinks our garments are now as fresh as
when we put them on first in Africa, at the
marriage of the King's daughter Claribel to the
King of Tunis.

SEBASTIAN

'Twas a sweet wedding, and marvelous feast,
but we hardly prosper in our return.

GONZALO

Sire, is not my doublet as fresh as when
I wore it at your daughter's marriage?

KING ALONSO

You cram these words into mine ears against
the stomach of my sense. My daughter is
married off far away, where I'm not likely to see
again, and now on our return, my only son, my
heir, is lost to briny depths unimaginable. Yet
you speak of miracles of clothing.

SEBASTIAN

My brother, your son may yet live.
I saw him beat the surges under him
and ride with confidence upon their backs.
I do not doubt that he could have landed safe.

KING ALONSO

No, no, he is gone.

GONZALO
Sir, I speak only to rouse you to our situation.
We are here. Must we not explore our chances?

(Enter Ariel and Spirits, playing somber music.)

KING ALONSO
My kingdom is without king nor heir, and we
are here … on a rock.

(Gonzalo falls asleep.)

What, he so soon asleep? I wish mine eyes
would … shut up my sorrowful thoughts …
mine most … heavy eyes.

(King Alonso sleeps. Ariel and Spirits exit.)

SEBASTIAN
What a strange drowsiness possesses them!

ANTONIO
It is the quality of the climate.

SEBASTIAN
Oh? I find myself not disposed to sleep.

ANTONIO
Nor I. I feel quite nimble.
They fell together all, as by consent.

Act 2 Scene 1

They dropped as by a thunderstroke. What
might, worthy and noble Sebastian, brother to
our King, what might this mean? – No more. --
And yet, methinks I see it in your face
what thou should'st be. The occasion speaks
thee, and my strong imagination sees a
crown dropping upon your head.

SEBASTIAN
What, art thou sleeping, too?

ANTONIO
Do you not hear me speak?

SEBASTIAN
(drawing his sword)
I do, and surely it is a sleepy language
you snore, or my ears mistake your intent,
for it is my brother who wears the crown.

ANTONIO
I am more serious than my custom. You
must be, too, if to heed this moment.

SEBASTIAN
What moment, sir?

ANTONIO
Oh, if you but knew how you the people cherish,
as the exalted general of all the King's armies.

SEBASTIAN
Prithee, say on.

ANTONIO
Thus, sir:
The Prince is gone.

SEBASTIAN
I have no hope that he's undrowned.

ANTONIO
Oh, out of that no hope,
what great hope have you! Will you grant with
me that Ferdinand is drowned?

SEBASTIAN
He's gone.

ANTONIO
Then tell me, who's the next heir of Naples?

SEBASTIAN
Claribel.

ANTONIO
She that is queen of Tunis; she that dwells
across the sea; she that from Naples
can have no note, unless the sun were post?
We all were sea-swallowed, though some cast
up again, and by that destiny to perform an act
whereof what's past is prologue, what to come
is yours and mine to discharge.

SEBASTIAN
What stuff is this? Claribel 'tis queen of Tunis,
and can be of Naples, also, despite the distance.

ANTONIO
A space between whose every inch
seems to cry out, "How shall that Claribel
measure us back to Naples? Keep in Tunis
and let Sebastian wake." Say this were death
that now hath seized them, why, here be he
that can rule Naples as well as he who sleeps.
There are other lords that can prate as amply
and as learnèd as this Gonzalo. Without boast,
I myself could help you there.
Oh, that you bore the mind that I do,
what a sleep were this for your advancement!
Do you understand me?

SEBASTIAN
Methinks I do.

ANTONIO
And how now to answer fortune?

SEBASTIAN
I remember, you did supplant your brother,
Prospero.

ANTONIO
True, and look how well my garments sit upon
me.

SEBASTIAN
But, for your conscience?

ANTONIO
Aye, sir, where lies that? I feel not such deity
in my bosom. Were there twenty consciences
that stood 'twixt me and Milan, so would they
have melted before me.
(drawing his sword)
Here lies your brother
whom I with this obedient steel, three inches of it,
can lay to bed forever; whiles you, doing thus,
might put steel to that perpetual yes-man.
For the rest, we shall live to tell of how the
tempest took their lives.

SEBASTIAN
Thy case, dear friend, shall be my precedent.
As thou got Milan, so shall I come by Naples.
Thrust thy sword. One stroke shall free thee
from the tribute which thou payest,
and I, the King, shall love thee for it.

ANTONIO
Draw together, and when I rear my hand,
do you the like to fall on Gonzalo.

*(They hold their swords
poised above King Alonso and
Gonzalo.)*

SEBASTIAN
Oh, but one word.

(They draw away to talk quietly. Ariel comes near to Gonzalo.)

ARIEL
While you here snoring lie,
open-eyed conspiracy its time doth take.
If of life you keep a care,
shake off slumber and beware!
Awake, awake!

(Antonio and Sebastian retake their positions.)

ANTONIO
Then let us both be sudden.

GONZALO
(waking and seeing their steel)
Good angels, preserve the King! My lord, awake!

KING ALONSO
(waking)
Why, how now? Sebastian, why are you drawn?

SEBASTIAN
Whiles we stood here, guarding your repose,
even now, we heard a hollow burst of bellowing

like bulls, or rather lions. Did it not wake you?

KING ALONSO
I heard nothing.

ANTONIO
Oh, 'twas a din to fright a monster's ear! A
roar, roaring sounds, as if a whole herd of lions.

KING ALONSO
Heard you this, Gonzalo?

GONZALO
Upon my honor, sir, I heard a humming,
and that a strange one, too, which did awake me.

KING ALONSO
Let us go forth from this place. All draw. Lead
on, brother Sebastian. Let's make further search
for my poor son.

ARIEL
Prospero my lord shall know what I have done.
So, king, go safely on to seek your son.

(They exit.)

SCENE 2

Another part of the island.

Enter Caliban carrying wood.

CALIBAN
All the infections that the sun sucks up,
from bogs, fens, flats, on Prosper fall and give him
by inchmeal a disease that rots his feet and shakes
his knees!

(Thunder crashes.)

Ah! His spirits hear me!
And yet I needs must curse. But
for every trifle are they set upon me,
sometimes like apes, that mow and chatter at me
and after bite me; then like hedgehogs, which
lie tumbling in my barefoot way and mount
their pricks at my footfall. Lo, now, lo!
even now, even as I'm already doing his errand,
here comes a spirit of his, and to torment me
for bringing wood in slowly. I'll fall flat.
Perchance he will not mind me.

(He lies down and covers himself with a cloak.)

Under here, I am out of sight.

(Enter Trinculo.)

TRINCULO
Here's neither bush nor shrub to bear off
any weather at all. And another storm brewing. I
hear it sing. If it should thunder as it did before, I
know not where to hide my head.
(noticing Caliban)
What have we here, a man or a fish? Dead or
alive? A fish; he smells like a fish – a very ancient
and fishlike smell, a kind of not-of-the-newest cod.
A strange fish. Were I in England, as once I was,
and had but this fish displayed, not a holiday
fool there but would give a piece of silver
to look upon such grotesque features.
Legged like a man, and his fins like
arms! Warm, by my troth! Say, I have an opinion.
which I'll let loose now: This is no fish, but an
islander that hath lately suffered by a thunderbolt.
(thunder crash)
Alas, the storm is come again. My best
way is to creep under his gaberdine. There is no
other shelter hereabout. Misery acquaints a man
with strange bedfellows. I will shelter here till the
dregs of the storm be past.

(He crawls under Caliban's cloak.

Enter Stephano.)

Act 2 Scene 2

STEPHANO

(singing, and drinking from a jug)

I shall no more to sea, to sea.
Here shall I die ashore, ashore.
Many fine maidens wait for me, for me.
Their wait will be long, for sure , for sure.

This is very scurvy tune to sing at a man's funeral. Well, here's to my comfort.

(drinks)

The master, the swabber, the boatswain, and I,
the gunner and his mate,
loved Moll, Meg, Mariam, and Margery,
but none of us cared for Kate.
For she had a tongue with a tang,
would cry to a sailor, "Go hang!"
She loved not the savor of tar nor of pitch,
yet a tailor might scratch her where'er she did itch.
Then to sea, boys, and let her go hang!
Then to sea, boys, and let her go hang!

This is a scurvy tune, too. But here's to my comfort.

(drinks)

CALIBAN

Oh! This is wrong!

STEPHANO

What's the matter? Have we devils here? Ha? I have not 'scaped drowning to be afeared now of your four legs.

Act 2 Scene 2

CALIBAN
The spirit torments me!

STEPHANO
This is some monster of the isle with four
legs. With that, I could fetch a guinea or two, if I
had some means to subdue it, some rope, and
a ship to get it home.

CALIBAN
Do not torment me, spirit. I will bring the
wood home faster. Oh, you are about to kill me!
I know it by your trembling.

STEPHANO
He's in a fit now. Come, open your mouth.
A jig o' this rum will settle you.
(He pours rum onto Caliban's face.)
Open your mouth, open! This will shake your
shaking, I can tell you, and that soundly.
(Caliban drinks.)

TRINCULO
I should know that voice. I do – but
he is drowned and it cannot be. These are devils!
Oh, God above, defend me!

STEPHANO
Four legs and two voices, a most tricky monster!
His forward voice is most thirsty.
(Caliban drinks more.)

Hold there, greedy monster, save some for us
other poor devils.
> *(He pulls the jug back from Caliban.)*

Thirsty you are, I will pour some in thy other
mouth.
> *(He pours into the cloak.)*

TRINCULO
Stephano!

STEPHANO
Does thy other mouth call me? Mercy, mercy,
this is a devil, and no monster! I will be away.

TRINCULO
Stephano! If thou be'st Stephano, touch me
and speak to me, for I am Trinculo – be not
afeard – thy good friend, Trinculo!

STEPHANO
What the devil? If any be Trinculo's legs,
these are they.
> *(He pulls Trinculo out.)*

Thou art very Trinculo indeed.
How is it you've found such a – ahem –
good friend? You and I just arrived on this isle.

TRINCULO
I took him to be killed with a thunderstroke.
But art thou not drowned, Stephano? I
hope now thou art not drowned. Is the storm

overblown? Oh, Stephano, we two Neapolitans
have survived when all else went down with the
ship.

STEPHANO
I know not how. When the blow came upon us,
I found several fine jugs in the master's larder,
friends indeed to a butler like me, who knows
the good stuff. The ship cracked open and out I
flowed, onto the sea! Me, and this good rum.
Floating with casks of this was my salvation.
(drinks)
How didst thou live? No other soul survived. If
you be real Trinculo, and not some vision else,
swear by this bottle how thou cam'st hither.

CALIBAN
I'll swear upon that bottle to be thy
true subject, for the liquor is not earthly.

TRINCULO
Swam ashore, man, like a duck. I can swim
like a duck.

STEPHANO
Here, warm your inside feathers, duck.

(Trinculo drinks.)

TRINCULO
Oh, Stephano, hast any more of this?

STEPHANO
The whole cask, man, and more. My cellar is a cave in a rock by the seaside. But how now, what are you?

CALIBAN
(emerging)
Hast thou not dropped from heaven?

STEPHANO
Out of the moon, I do assure you. I was the man i' the moon when time was.

CALIBAN
I have seen thee in her, and I adore thee!

STEPHANO
(holding out the jug)
Come, swear to that. Kiss the book. I will furnish it anon with new contents.

(Caliban drinks.)

TRINCULO
By this good light, this is a very shallow monster.

CALIBAN
I'll show thee every fertile inch o' th' island, and I will kiss thy foot. I prithee, be my god.

STEPHANO
Come on, then. Down and swear. Swear your
allegiance, island monster.

(Caliban kneels.)

CALIBAN
I'll show thee the best springs. I'll
fish for thee and get thee wood enough.
A plague upon the tyrant that I serve.
I'll bear him no more sticks, but follow you.

TRINCULO
A most ridiculous monster, to make a wonder
of a poor drunkard.

CALIBAN
(standing)
I prithee, let me bring thee where crabs grow.

STEPHANO
Well, fine. Trinculo, the King and all our company
else being drowned, we will inherit here.
Here, be my bottle-bearer. Fellow Trinculo, we'll
fill him by and by again.

CALIBAN
(singing drunkenly)
Farewell, master, farewell, farewell.

TRINCULO
A howling monster, a drunken monster.

CALIBAN

No more dams I'll make for fish
nor fetch in firing
at requiring,
nor scrape trenchering, nor wash dish,
'ban, 'ban, Ca-caliban
has a new master. Get a new man!

STEPHANO and TRINCULO
(sharing the jug)

Get a new man!
Get a new man!

STEPHANO
(drinking the last of the jug)
This soldier is dead. Come, back to my house.

(They exit.)

ACT 3

SCENE 1

Before Prospero's home, Prospero sits with his book in a hidden spot.

Enter Ferdinand, carrying a log.

FERDINAND
There be some sports are painful, and their labor
delight in them sets off; some kinds of baseness
are nobly undergone. This my mean task
would be as heavy to me, as odious, but
the mistress which I serve quickens what's dead,
and makes my labors pleasures. Oh, she is
ten times more gentle than her father's crabbed.
I must remove some thousands of these logs and
pile them up. My sweet mistress
weeps when she sees me work, and says never
has anyone done so well.

(Enter Miranda.)

MIRANDA
Alas now, pray you,

work not so hard. My father
is gone at study, away where he can't see you.
We're safe for these three hours.

FERDINAND

Oh, most dear mistress,
the sun will set ere I am able to move
these heavy logs, as I must do.

MIRANDA

If you'll sit down, I'll bear your logs for the while.
Pray, give me that. I'll carry it to the pile.

FERDINAND

No, precious creature, 'tis too heavy for you.
I had rather crack my sinews, break my back,
than you should such mighty burden attempt.

MIRANDA

It would become me, and I should do it,
for my good will is to it, and yours against.

*(She picks up a log and
carries it to the pile.)*

PROSPERO
(aside)
Poor worm, thou art infected.
This visitation proves it.

Act 3 Scene 1

MIRANDA
(returning)
You look weary.

FERDINAND
No, noble mistress, 'tis fresh morning with me
when you are by at night. I do beseech you,
chiefly that I might set it in my prayers,
what is your name?

MIRANDA
Miranda. – Oh, my father said not to say so!

FERDINAND
Admired Miranda!
Indeed the top of admiration, worth
what's dearest to the world! Oh, you,
so perfect and so peerless, are created
of every creature's best.

MIRANDA
I do not know one of my sex,
and you are the only real man I've met,
but I would not wish any companion
in the world but you. But I prattle
something too wildly.

FERDINAND
The very instant that I saw you did
my heart fly to your service, there resides
to make me slave to it, and for your sake
am I this patient log-man.

Act 3 Scene 1

MIRANDA
Do you love me?

FERDINAND
Oh, heaven, oh, earth, bear witness to this sound.
I, beyond all limit of what else in the world,
do love, prize and honor you.

MIRANDA
I am a fool
to weep at what I am glad of.

PROSPERO
(aside)
Fair encounter of two most rare affections.
Heavens rain grace on that which breeds between 'em!

FERDINAND
Wherefore weep you?

MIRANDA
At mine unworthiness, that dare not offer
what I desire to give, and much less take
what I shall die to want. Oh, fie all bashfulness.
I am your wife if you will marry me.

FERDINAND
My mistress, dearest, and I thus humble ever.

MIRANDA
My husband, then?

FERDINAND
Aye, with a heart as willing as bondage e'er
o'ertook freedom. Here's my hand.

MIRANDA
And mine, with my heart in it. And now come
inside, for half an hour, at the least. We
have piles of dollop berries, for your feast.

FERDINAND
If by your hand picked, they must be good,
indeed.

(They exit.)

PROSPERO
From foolish love comes heady life;
I must watch closely ere it do so.
Miranda, my daughter, the extension of my life;
she is my legacy. Oh, cruel brother of mine,
who would cut off her life, how you shall suffer!
Yet, for the nonce, I do believe I shall find a nook
to read my book, and mayhap nap me.

(He exits.)

SCENE 2

Part of the island.

Enter King Alonso, Sebastian, Antonio, Gonzalo, crossing.

KING ALONSO
This way, men. Let us look over here.

GONZALO
More green grass; the isle is full of it,
which portends well, for green is a joyous color.

ANTONIO
Yippee. My heart rejoices for grass.

SEBASTIAN
There is no sign of my nephew anywhere.
He swam mightily and would not have
succumbed any easier than we. –
But, methinks perhaps, he swam thataway, out
to sea.

ANTONIO
(aside to Sebastian)
The Prince is gone, and you should be king!

(They exit.

Enter Caliban, Stephano and Trinculo.)

CALIBAN
Master, I can take you to the freshest springs,
where crystal clean water flows year 'round.

(Stephano reveals his hidden cache of rum casks.)

STEPHANO
Water? Ha, when the casks are
dry, we will drink water, not a drop before.
Therefore, bear up and board 'em. Servant
monster, drink to me.

TRINCULO
Servant monster? The folly of this island!

STEPHANO
Drink, servant monster, when I bid thee.

(Caliban drinks.)

STEPHANO
We leaders must govern. You, monster, I
shall make a lieutenant, or general.

TRINCULO
Your lieutenant, if you list. He's no general.

STEPHANO
Mooncalf, speak, if thou be'st a good mooncalf.

CALIBAN
How does thy Honor? Let me lick your shoe. I'll not serve him; he is not valiant.

TRINCULO
Thou liest, most ignorant monster. I have been King Alonso's steward for many long years. I know better how to govern than any half-fish half-monster man-thing fish.

CALIBAN
Lo, how he mocks me! Wilt thou let him, my lord?

TRINCULO
"Lord" is it?

CALIBAN
Lo, lo, again! Bite him to death, I prithee.

STEPHANO
Trinculo, keep a good tongue in your head. If you prove a mutineer, the next tree. This poor monster is my subject.

CALIBAN
I thank you, noble lord. Wilt thou be pleased to harken once again to the suit I made to thee?

STEPHANO
Yes, but repeat it. I may have been drinking
when you before laid it out to me.

(He drinks.

Enter Ariel and Spirits.)

CALIBAN
As I told you, I am subject to a tyrant, a
sorcerer, that stole this island from me.

ARIEL
(in Trinculo's voice)

Thou liest!

CALIBAN
(to Trinculo)
Thou liest, thou jesting monkey, thou!

STEPHANO
Trinculo, if you trouble him any more in 's
tale, by this hand, I will supplant some of your
teeth.

TRINCULO
Why, I said nothing.

STEPHANO
Mum then, and say no more.

(Trinculo moves aside.)

CALIBAN
I say, by sorcery he got this isle, from me.
I will serve you, and show you how you mayst
knock a nail into his head.

ARIEL
(in Trinculo's voice)
Thou liest. Thou canst not.

CALIBAN
What a pied ninny's this! Thou scurvy patch!
I do beseech your Greatness, give him blows
and take his bottle from him.

STEPHANO
Trinculo, run into no further danger.

TRINCULO
Why, what did I? I did nothing. I'll go
farther off.

STEPHANO
Didst thou not say he lied?

ARIEL
(in Trinculo's voice)
Thou liest.

STEPHANO
Do I so? Take thou that.

(He beats Trinculo.)

TRINCULO
I did not give the lie! Lay off! I did nothing!

CALIBAN
Ha, ha, ha!

STEPHANO
Now, forward with your tale.

CALIBAN
Beat him enough. After a little time
I'll beat him, too.

STEPHANO
(to Trinculo)
Stand farther.

CALIBAN
'Tis a custom with the sorcerer i' th'
afternoon to sleep. There thou mayst brain him,
having first seized his books. Remember this!
First to possess his books, for without them
he's but a sot, as I am, and has not
one spirit to command. They all hate him.
Burn out his books and he will have nothing,
save the beauty of his daughter.
He himself calls her "nonpareil", a "bright
exemplar of femalehood," though I've seen no
others and do not myself know for certain to

compare.

STEPHANO
Is it so brave a lass?

CALIBAN
Aye, lord, she will become thy bed, I warrant,
and bring thee forth brave brood.

STEPHANO
Monster, I will kill this man. His daughter
and I will be king and queen – you may bow! –
and Trinculo and thyself shall be viceroys. –
Dost thou like the plot, Trinculo?

TRINCULO
Excellent.

STEPHANO
Give me thy hand. I am sorry I beat thee.

CALIBAN
Within this half hour will he be asleep.
Wilt thou destroy him then?

STEPHANO
Aye, on mine honor.

ARIEL
(aside)
This will I tell my master.

(Ariel and Spirits play music, dance around the bewildered men, and exit.)

TRINCULO
This is a marvelous odd island, indeed.

CALIBAN
Be not afeard. The isle is full of noises,
sounds and sweet airs that give delight and hurt
not.

STEPHANO
I will be king and get my music for free. Come!

(They exit.)

SCENE 3

Another part of the island.

Enter King Alonso, Sebastian, Antonio, and Gonzalo.

KING ALONSO
Halt, here. I fear we travel in circles
for these rocks all look so alike, and my
heart is full of deep despair. Certain am I that
he is drownèd whom thus we stray to find, and

the sea mocks our frustrated search on land.
Sit down, all, for I must rest.

ANTONIO
(aside to Sebastian)
I am right glad that he's so out of hope.
Do not forget your purpose, Sire.

SEBASTIAN
(to Antonio)
The next advantage will we take decisively.

ANTONIO
(to Sebastian)
Tonight? For after this they will sleep soundly
with little chance of diligence.

SEBASTIAN
(to Antonio)
I say tonight. No more.

(Strange and solemn music, and enter Prospero on the top invisible.)

KING ALONSO
Hark! Do others hear this?

GONZALO
Marvelous sweet music!

Act 3 Scene 3

(Enter the Spirits, shrouded in strange shapes, bearing a feast which they place in front of the men and then dance.)

KING ALONSO
Am I dead? What are these?

SEBASTIAN
Valhalla? Heaven? Now will I believe
that there are unicorns, that in Arabia
there sits a phoenix on a golden throne, and in
Scotland a beast in Loch Ness.

ANTONIO
I'll believe it all.

GONZALO
If back in Naples I should report this now,
would they believe me?
If I should say I saw such islanders –
for certain, these are people of the island –
who, though they are of monstrous shape, yet note
their manners are more gentle than your European,
than of your civilized sort, for they are not yet so
ruined.

PROSPERO
(aside)
Honest Lord, thou hast said well, for some here
present are worse than devils.

Act 3 Scene 2

(The Spirits fade away.)

SEBASTIAN
They vanish strangely, yet see
what foods they have left behind.
All types of wondrous dishes! Will you
eat, Sire?

KING ALONSO
I do hunger, for last night's dinner was long
before last night's storm. But hold; this may be
not safe.

GONZALO
Faith, sir, you need not fear. This has all,
I'm certain, been offered as a welcome blessing
from the primitive island natives,
who are happy to celebrate our arrival.

(Thunder and lightning. Gonzalo withdraws to the side. Enter Ariel, dressed as a Harpy, claps his wings, and the feast vanishes.)

ARIEL
(as Harpy)
You are three men of sin, whom Destiny
hath caused to belch up upon this island
of spirits, where man doth not inhabit.
You three are enemies to harmony and deserve
most horrendous and vile punishment.

I have made you mad, in hopes you might,
like proper men, hang and drown yourselves.

> *(King Alonso, Sebastian and
> Antonio draw their swords.
> They attack, but can't hit
> anything. Spirits return and
> swirl around them.)*

ARIEL
You fools! I and my fellows
are ministers of fate. The elements
of whom your swords are tempered may as well
wound the loud winds or with bemocked-at stabs
kill the still-closing waters as diminish
one iota of my presence. My fellow ministers
are like invulnerable. Besides, your swords grow
now too massy for your strengths, and will not
be uplifted.

> *(The men drop their swords.)*

ARIEL
But remember – for that's my business to you –
that you three did supplant good Prospero,
exposed unto the sea, him and his innocent child,
for which foul deed the Powers – not forgetting –
have incensed the seas and shores against you.
Revenge and justice, most sweet at last.
Thee of thy son, Alonso, they have bereft, and
for you three vile men have in store
that which would curdle any mortal's milk.

Despair, despair, despair!

(He vanishes in thunder.)

PROSPERO
(aside)
Bravely done, Ariel. Let them stew on that, whilst they starve along the barren seashore, and in these fits will I leave them.

(He exits.)

GONZALO
(coming forward)
In the name of something holy, sir, why so you stand in this strange stare?

KING ALONSO
Oh, it is monstrous, monstrous!
Methought the wind did speak, and
the thunder, that deep and dreadful organ pipe,
did say the name of "Prospero."
Therefor is my son in the mud imbedded, and
for my crimes, therefor will I follow him there.

(He exits.)

SEBASTIAN
(picking up his sword and the King's)
To arms, to arms! There is a legion of them, and we must fight!

ANTONIO
(picking up his sword)

I'll be thy second!

(Sebastian and Antonio exit.)

GONZALO

Well. They seem most desperate.
This humid salt-filled ocean air is known to
affect the psyche in strange and wondrous ways.

(He picks up and nibbles at some remaining food.)

Oh, my. Why, this is just a stick painted to look like food. –
I will follow my mad friends, to keep them sane,
though I fear we all may be too far gone, already.

(He exits.)

ACT 4

SCENE 1

Before Prospero's home.

Enter Miranda and Ferdinand.

MIRANDA
Here, of course. We shall live together
here, on this island, with father!
What troubles you, dearest Ferdie?
Do not you love me?

FERDINAND
Oh, more than ever, more than ships
love to frolic over waves, rather than beneath
them. I had just hoped –

MIRANDA
Hoped what?

FERDINAND
That perhaps we could find a happy ship
and make our way home.

Act 4 Scene 1

MIRANDA
I am home.

(Enter Prospero.)

PROSPERO
(to Ferdinand)
If I have too austerely punished you,
your compensation more than makes amends,
for I am giving you here a third of mine own life.

(Noting their surliness.)

But what gives? Do you not wish to proceed?

FERDINAND
Oh, yes, sir! Yes, I do! I do! I say it, I do!

MIRANDA
Are you certain?

FERDINAND
Never more so!

MIRANDA
Then yes, father.

PROSPERO
Very well. Then, as my gift, take my daughter,
she is yours. But if thou dost break her virgin-knot
before all sanctimonious ceremonies may with full
and holy rite be ministered, no sweet blessings

Act 4 Scene 1

shall save you. Barren discord shall bestrew
the union of your bed with weeds so loathly
that you shall hate it both. Therefore, take heed,
as Hymen's lamps shall light you.

FERDINAND

As I do hope
for quiet days, fair issue, long life,
with such love as 'tis now, my lust shall I
reign in place, hitched tightly, as if with sturdy
rope and no scissors near, a balloon unpopped,
a mighty whale with tail tied to immovable rocks,
cast iron clamps with grips so tightly wound, no
air or e'en light between the jaws.

PROSPERO

Uh, yes. -- Sit then and talk with her. Get used to
that. The festivities will begin shortly.

(Ferdinand and Miranda withdraw.)

PROSPERO

What, Ariel, my industrious servant, Ariel!

(Enter Ariel.)

ARIEL

Here I am, master.

PROSPERO

Are your players ready?

ARIEL
Is now the time to doubt us, master?

PROSPERO
Begin then.

(Soft music. Enter Iris.)

IRIS
Ceres, most bounteous lady, leas
of wheat, rye, barley, oats and peas;
thy turfy mountains, where live nibbling sheep,
and flat meadows filled with hay, them to keep;
thy verdant over-flowing vineyard,
and thy seashore, sterile and rocky hard,
where thou thyself dost air – the Queen o' th' sky,
whose watery luscious messenger am I,
bids thee come and sport in this port. Approach,
rich Ceres, her to please.

(Enter Ceres.)

CERES
Hail, many-colored messenger, that ne'er
dost disobey the wife of Jupiter. Why hath thy queen
summoned me hither, to this short-grassed green?

IRIS
We come to this fine estate, for
a contract of true love to celebrate.

Act 4 Scene 1

CERES
These two here, who sit with in'twined fingers?
Love, deep enough, though mem'ry stale lingers
of storm and force, on one, th 'other naïve.
Here be manipulations, I believe.

IRIS
With cause, sweet Ceres, golden flower,
and with never an abuse of power,
for these innocent younglings have bound
themselves together on their own grounds,
of wills ever free from confusion,
although their meeting came from fusion
of those at sea in passing king's ship
with those on shore thrown out from kinship.

(Juno descends.)

CERES
Highest queen of state,
great Juno, comes.

IRIS
We celebrate!

JUNO
How does my bounteous sister? Sing with me
to bless this twain, that they may prosperous be.

(They sing.)

Act 4 Scene 1

JUNO
Honor, riches, marriage-blessing
long continuance and increasing,
hourly joy be loud upon you.
Juno sings her blessings on you.

CERES
Earth's increase, pleasure plenty,
barns and larders never empty,
vines with clust'ring bunches growing,
plants with goodly burden bowing;
scarcity and want shall shun you,
Ceres' blessing so is on you.

FERDINAND
This is some majestic vision. May I
be bold to think these spirits?

PROSPERO
Spirits, which by my art
have I from their confines called to bless
your union with my daughter.

FERDINAND
Then, father, and glorious new bride,
let me live here forever.
This place is a paradise.

PROSPERO
Hush now, our spell has been marred.
The time has come for that foul conspiracy
of the beast Caliban and his confederates

against my life. The minute of their plot
is almost come. – Well done. Avoid. No more.

(The Spirits vanish.)

FERDINAND
(to Miranda)
This is strange. Your father's in some passion
that works him strongly.

MIRANDA
Never till this day saw I ever
him touched so with anger, so distempered.

PROSPERO
The time has come for the full power of
my art to lash out at those who would harm us!

MIRANDA
Father, surely there is some other way? Violent
harm does harm more to he who strikes.

PROSPERO
You do both look as if you are dismayed.
Be cheerful. Our revels now are ended. These
our actors, as I foretold you, were all spirits and
are melted into air, into thin air;
and like the baseless fabric of this vision,
everything, this seemingly solid world,
yea, all which it inherit, shall dissolve,
and, like this insubstantial pageant faded,
leave not a crumb behind. We are such stuff

as dreams are made on, and our little life
is rounded with a sleep. My old brain is troubled.
Leave me, young lovebirds; go inside
and there repose. A turn or two I'll walk
to clear my beating mind.

    FERDINAND / MIRANDA
We wish you peace.

(They exit.)

    PROSPERO
Come with a thought, clever helper.

(Enter Ariel.)

    ARIEL
Thy thoughts I cleave to. What's thy pleasure?

    PROSPERO
We must prepare to meet with Caliban.

    ARIEL
I have led them most horribly, my master,
as you my feet have instructed.
First, to follow my music, charmed calf-like,
through toothèd briars, sharp stickers, pricking
gorse, and thorns, which entered their frail shins.
At last I left them i' th' filthy-mantled pool,
there sinking up to their chins, that the foul lake
o'erstunk their feet.

Act 4 Scene 1

PROSPERO
Oh, yes. This was well done, my bird. Now, go
fetch ye the trumpery in my house and
bring it hither, for more to play upon them.

ARIEL
I go, I go.

(He exits.)

PROSPERO
Brain me, would they?
I will plague them all, even to roaring.
Although, it is my pain which speaks out loud
while my reason calls its due in stifled whisper.

(Enter Ariel and Spirits, carrying glistening apparel.)

PROSPERO
Come, hang them on this line.

(Enter Caliban, Stephano, and Trinculo, all wet, as Prospero and Ariel look on.)

CALIBAN
Pray you, tread softly. We are now near his cell.

STEPHANO
Monster, your fairy, which you say is a
harmless fairy, has done little better than played

the jack with us.

TRINCULO
Monster, I do smell all horse piss, at which
my nose is in great indignation.

STEPHANO
So is mine. – Do you hear, monster?

TRINCULO
Thou wert but a lost monster.

CALIBAN
Good, my lord, give me thy favor still.
We are here. Therefore speak softly.
All's hushed as midnight yet.

TRINCULO
Aye, but to lose our bottles in the pond!

STEPHANO
An infinite loss. Mayhap we should return --

CALIBAN
Oh, prithee, my king, be quiet. Seest thou here,
this is the mouth o' th' cell. No noise, and enter.
Do that good mischief which may take this isle,
and its flowing streams and berry patches, and
the sorcerer's unplucked daughter, are all yours.

STEPHANO
I do begin to have bloody thoughts.

(The Spirits reveal the line of shiny clothing.)

TRINCULO
Oh, King Stephano, oh
peer, oh worthy Stephano, look what wardrobe
here is for thee!

CALIBAN
Let it alone, fool. It is but trash.

TRINCULO
Oh ho, monster, this is quality.
              (putting on one of the gowns)
Oh, King Stephano!

STEPHANO
Put off that gown, Trinculo. By this hand,
I'll have that gown.

TRINCULO
Thy Grace shall have it.

CALIBAN
The dropsy drown this fool! What do you mean
to dote thus on such luggage? Let it alone,
and do the murder first.

STEPHANO
Be you quiet, monster. Trinculo, this jerkin
be of stunningly clever stitching.

TRINCULO
'Tis fit for a king, and none of it smells horsey.

STEPHANO
In my realm, everyone shall wear such finery, as befits their station. You, sir, oh, yes that quite becomes you. Monster, try this on.

CALIBAN
I'll none of it. We shall lose our time
and all be turned to barnacles or to apes
with foreheads villainous low.

TRINCULO
There is so much treasure here!

STEPHANO
Monster, lay to your fingers. Help to bear this away. We shall retire back to where my hogshead of rum is. Go to, carry this.

TRINCULO
And this.

STEPHANO
And this.

CALIBAN
But first, do the murder!

Act 4 Scene 1

(A noise of baying hounds is heard.)

PROSPERO
Hey, Mountain, hey!

ARIEL
Silver! There they are! Get 'em, Silver!

(Enter Spirits in shapes of dogs, to chase the men about.)

PROSPERO
Go, Fury, go Whirlwind! Get them!

STEPHANO
Hell hounds, or I'll not know the difference!

TRINCULO
Monster, hold tight! Don't lose the frippery!

CALIBAN
Run, master!

(They exit, with the Spirit hounds pursuing.)

ARIEL
Hark, how they roar.

PROSPERO
Go. Let them be hunted soundly, but keep your

spirits from doing lasting damage.
At this hour lies at my mercy all mine enemies.
Shortly shall all my labors end, and thou
shalt have the air at freedom. Go, do as I say,
for but a short time longer.

(They exit.)

ACT 5

SCENE 1

Before Prospero's home.

Enter Ariel and Prospero, with Spirits around.

ARIEL
Master, have you forgotten the one called
"King" and his men, whom at your instruction
I did there leave them all, prisoners, sir,
in the line grove which weather-fends your cell?
They cannot budge till your release. The King,
his brother, and yours abide all three distracted,
and the other mourning over them,
brimful of sorrow and dismay; but chiefly
him that you termed, sir, the "good old lord Gonzalo" –
his tears run down his cheek like winter's drops.
Your charm so strongly works 'em that if you
now beheld them, your affection would become tender.

PROSPERO
Do you think so, spirit?

ARIEL
Mine would, sir, were I human.

PROSPERO
And mine shall.
You, spirit, can show compassion that wouldst
of humanity alone be expected. Am I so hard?
These men exiled me here to this isle, stranded
me here with my daughter, yet am I so harmed
that I must let vengeance muck my nobler reason?
The rarer action is in virtue than in vengeance.
Be they penitent, the purpose of my tempest
does extend not a frown further. Go, release
them, Ariel.
My charms I'll break, their senses I'll restore,
and they shall be themselves.

ARIEL
I'll fetch them, sir.

(He exits.)

PROSPERO
You spirits of hills, brooks, standing lakes and
rocks,
you demi-puppets that by moonshine dance and
play,
you elemental powers underlying day and
night,
by whose aid I've gained my powerful art, and
learned to move heaven and earth; to stir the
winds and sea to do my bidding; to open graves

and wake their sleepers; to befuddle minds of
fools and great thinkers alike -- hear me now.

*(Prospero draws a large circle
on the ground with his staff.)*

Once more, my art, but this once, for
when I'm done, I will break my staff,
bury it certain fathoms in the earth,
and even deeper shall I drown my book.

*(Enter Ariel, leading King
Alonso, Gonzalo, Sebastian,
and Antonio, all in a daze.
They enter the circle and
stand charmed.)*

PROSPERO

There stand, for you are spell-stopped.
You there, Gonzalo, honorable man,
with your kindness you did save Miranda and
me; a kindness remembered. Oh, good Gonzalo,
my true preserver and a loyal sir
to him thou follow'st, I will reward thy graces,
both in word and deed. – Most cruelly
did you, Alonso, use me and my daughter.
Thy brother was a furtherer in the act. –
And you, brother mine, that took all from me,
that worshipped ambition over brotherly love.
Yet I forgive thee all. –
The spell begins to dissipate, and their
understanding swells, yet still they do not

recognize me in my robes of magic art.
Ariel, fetch me my old attire, as I was
sometime in Milan.

> *(Ariel exits and returns with garments. He helps Prospero change.)*

PROSPERO
Quickly, spirit; thou shalt ere long be free.

ARIEL
(singing)
Merrily, merrily shall I live now
under the blossom that hangs on the bough.

SPIRITS
(singing)
Merrily, merrily shall we live now
under the blossom that hangs on the bough.

> *(The Spirits make a pile of Prospero's magic robe and garments.)*

PROSPERO
(now dressed as the Duke of Milan)
My dainty Ariel, I shall miss thee, but yet
thou shall have your freedom. Now, to the
King's ship, to wake the mariners asleep
under the hatches. The master and the mate,

being awake, guide them here, I prithee.

ARIEL

Faster than your pulse twice beat.

(He exits.)

GONZALO
(seeing Prospero)

All torment, trouble, wonder, and amazement
inhabits here. – Are you not my old friend,
Prospero?

PROSPERO
(to King Alonso)

Behold, sir King,
the wrongèd Duke of Milan, Prospero.
For more assurance that a living prince
does now speak to thee, I embrace thy body,
(he hugs King Alonso)
and to thee and thy company I bid
a hearty welcome.

KING ALONSO

Are you indeed real? Thy pulse
beats as of flesh and blood. Yet I fear
a madness held me, from which I slowly wake.
Prospero! If this be you, a most strange story must
be yours, that you live. Thy dukedom I resign, and
now give back to you. Yet tell us, how should
Prospero be living, and be found here?

Act 5 Scene 1

PROSPERO
(to Gonzalo)
First, noble friend, let me embrace you.

GONZALO
Whether this be real or be not, I'll not swear.

PROSPERO
You do yet taste
some subtleties of the isle, that will not let you
believe things certain. Welcome, my friends all.
*(aside to Sebastian and
Antonio)*
But you, my brace of lords, should I bespeak you
traitors?

ANTONIO
(aside to Sebastian)
He knows!

SEBASTIAN
(aside)
The devil speaks in him.

PROSPERO
(aside)
No. But you, brother, I do forgive thy rankest
fault, so long as you restore my dukedom to me.

ANTONIO
Brother! I, I am ... astounded to hear you still call
me "brother." Your rightful place is yours again. I

thank you, for your leniency and mercy.

KING ALONSO

If you be Prospero,
give us particulars of thy preservation,
how thou hast met us here, whom three hours ago
were wrecked upon this shore, where I have lost
my dear son, the prince, my Ferdinand.

PROSPERO

Does it seem three hours to you? And yet,
a lifetime to me. I have suffered your same loss, sir.

KING ALONSO

You, the same loss?

PROSPERO

I have lost my daughter, sir.

KING ALONSO

A daughter? Oh, heavens, that they both lived.
They could be king and queen in Naples, and I
instead mudded in that oozy bed
where my son lies! – When did you lose your
daughter?

PROSPERO

In this tempest. Pray you, since you have
my dukedom given me again, I will
requite you with as good a thing to content
you as much as me my dukedom.

Act 5 Scene 1

(Prospero unveils Ferdinand and Miranda playing chess.)

MIRANDA
(to Ferdinand)
My sweet lord, methinks you play me false.

FERDINAND
No, my dearest love, so goes the knight.

KING ALONSO
What hoped-for vision is this?

FERDINAND
(rising upon seeing King Alonso)
The seas are merciful! I have cursed them without cause.

KING ALONSO
(embracing him)
My son! Now, all the blessing of a glad father on thee!

MIRANDA
(coming forward)
Oh, wonder! How many goodly creatures are there here!

PROSPERO
I hope you are satisfied with the one.

KING ALONSO
(to Ferdinand)
What is this maid with whom thou wast at play?
Is she the goddess that has separated us
and thus bewitched you?

FERDINAND
Sir, she is mortal,
but by immortal providence she's mine.
I chose her when I could not ask my father
for his advice, nor thought I had one. She
is daughter to this famous Duke of Milan,
of whom I have received a second life, and
now second father have I received.

KING ALONSO
(to Prospero)
And I second life and second son.

PROSPERO
And second daughter.

KING ALONSO
I am forever in your debt, sir.

GONZALO
This is most glorious. Look down, you
gods, and on this couple drop a blessèd crown.

KING ALONSO
I say "Amen", Gonzalo.

Act 5 Scene 1

GONZALO
Was Milan thrust from Milan, that his issue
should become kings of Naples? Oh, rejoice
beyond a common joy: in one voyage
did Claribel her husband find at Tunis,
and Ferdinand, her brother, found a wife
where he himself was lost; Prospero his
dukedom, and all of us ourselves when no man
was his own.

(Enter Ariel with the Captain and First Mate.)

GONZALO
Oh, look, Sire, here is more of us. What
is the news?

FIRST MATE
The best news is that we have safely found
our king and company. The next: our ship,
which, but three glasses since, we saw wrecked
and split, is tight and yar and bravely rigged as
when we first put out to sea.

ARIEL
(aside to Prospero)
Sir, all this service have I done since I went.

PROSPERO
(aside to Ariel)
My tricksy spirit!

Act 5 Scene 1

KING ALONSO

These are not natural events. They strengthen
from strange to stranger. Good mariners, how
came you to find us hither?

FIRST MATE

If I could, sir, I'd strive to tell you. Even
now, it swims in my mem'ry.
We were awaked, from where we oddly slept
in the holds, and in a trice found ourselves
on deck, work in hand to set the sails.

CAPTAIN

Good Sire, our ship leapt o'er waves as if alive,
moreso even than we, and here to these shores
we found us almost before we fully awoke.

ARIEL
(aside to Prospero)

Was 't well done?

PROSPERO
(aside to Ariel)

Bravely, my diligence. You have almost earned
your freedom, but now go and seek thee the rest.
Untie the spell and bring them here.

(Ariel exits.)

PROSPERO
(to King Alonso)

My liege, do not give worry to the strangeness of

these airy events. This isle is a magical place, of powers old and elemental, and best forgotten. Be cheerful of these happy accidents.
But good King, there are yet missing of your company some very odd lads, as you might recall.

(Enter Ariel, driving in Caliban, Stephano and Trinculo in their stolen garments.)

STEPHANO
Ow! By heavens, what is this pestilence? It stings! It drives me hither! Every man for himself, stand not on ceremony!

TRINCULO
(seeing King Alonso and company)
Oh! – Oh. Hello.

PROSPERO
This misshapen knave, his mother was a witch, who died long ago and left him on this isle. These three have robbed me, and plotted to take my life. Two of these fellows you must know and own. This thing of darkness, I acknowledge mine.

CALIBAN
I shall be pinched to death.

Act 5 Scene 1

KING ALONSO
Is this not Stephano, my drunken butler?

SEBASTIAN
He is drunk even now. Where had he wine?

KING ALONSO
And Trinculo, my steward, and reeling ripe.
How cam'st thou, Trinculo, in this pickle?

TRINCULO
I am in such a pickle.

SEBASTIAN
How now, Stephano?

STEPHANO
Oh, my head! I have been drugged most foul by
magic pestilence! By your honor, my lord,
and for your honor, at great personal risk
and against mighty travails, when all was lost
and foundering upon the evil rocks, I
safeguarded a cask, or two, saved them from
certain drowning in the angry sea. 'Twas my
duty, and I'd be embarrassed to be thanked, or
be-ribboned for my gallantry.

TRINCULO
I helped him.

Act 5 Scene 1

          KING ALONSO
                (indicating Caliban)
This is as strange a thing as ever I did look upon.

          PROSPERO
He was born upon and of this isle.
                (to Caliban)
Caliban, do not shake. Go you to my cell. Take
your companions and make everything good
there, if you are clever enough to seek my
pardon.

          CALIBAN
Aye, that I will, and I'll be wise hereafter
and seek for grace. What a thrice-double ass
was I, to take this drunkard for a god!

                *(Caliban, Stephano and
                Trinculo exit.)*

          PROSPERO
Good sir, King Alonso, there is one thing more.
I beg you do this revealing play observe:

                *(Prospero waves his staff at
                Antonio and Sebastian.)*

          ANTONIO
                (unable to stop his words)
Sebastian, sire, tonight when guard is down,
we are free to kill the King and give you his
crown.

SEBASTIAN
(also unable to stop his words)

Yes, that is my plan precisely, for then my brother would ne'er see it coming and we can tell all he and Gonzalo both fell stricken, victims of this unfortunate tempest.

(Sebastian and Antonio fall to their knees before King Alonso.)

KING ALONSO

Give up your swords, vile traitors, brother of mine and brother of Prospero. I'll have your heads for this.

PROSPERO

My King, surely mercy and forgiveness beget mercy and forgiveness.

KING ALONSO

Wisely said, sir Duke of Milan.
(to Sebastian and Antonio)
Very well. Upon our return you shall live, but how you shall live will be further discussed.

GONZALO

Sire, if I may be so bold as this to suggest, that your army captains are ever in need of lieutenants, of rank and file so low.

Act 5 Scene 1

KING ALONSO
Fantastic. Make it so. And you, Gonzalo,
long have I underrated your loyal counsel,
and now give you my brother's position:
you shall be general to all my troops.

PROSPERO
Sir, I invite your Highness and your train
to take your rest and find some refreshments
in my humble home. Rest the night, part of
which will I fill with the story of my life, and
in the morn I'll bring you to your ship, and
so shall we all to Naples, where I hope to
see the nuptials of these our dear-belovèd
children solemnized, and thence retire me to
my Milan.

KING ALONSO
I long to hear your story, which must
take the ear strangely.

PROSPERO
I'll deliver all, and promise you calm seas
and sail so expeditious that we shall catch your
fleet.
(to Ariel)
Ariel, my sweet, that is thy last charge. Then, to
the elements, be free, and fare thou well.

ARIEL
Ah! Blessèd master. To the winds go I!
(He exits.)

Act 5 Scene 1

PROSPERO
Come, my liege, come all. Dine with me, in my humble abode, and with me wish blessings upon this fruitful couple.

MIRANDA
Oh, do come in, all. We have needle berries, morgendish fruit and to drink, the sweetest fernroot wine.

FERDINAND
Isn't she a wonder!

(All exit, but Prospero and Spirits.

Prospero causes a pit to open, over which he holds his staff, then breaks it and throws the pieces into the pit.)

The Spirits hand him his magical garments, which he holds high, then hands back. The Spirits hold them high, and then drop them into the pit.

Prospero holds up his treasured book of spells, holds it high, and then drops it into the pit. With its destruction, the Spirits caper away and exit.)

EPILOGUE

Prospero comes forward,
dressed plainly.

PROSPERO
Oh, spirits of this world and that!
Now stand I before you freely, without
pretension of office or art, just me, and
beg your understanding, even your forgiving.
Now my charms are all o'erthrown,
and what strength I have is mine own,
which is most faint. My time is passing.
Now let the next generation
play upon our fields, for right or wrong, good
and evil, well intentioned and not. I've played
my turn, the rest of my days to sit on the sides
and but observe both folly and wise.
Remember me well.

(He exits.)

CURTAINS.

Notes

Character Notes

You've been cast! Hoorah! Now, before fame and glory, roses and chocolate, steak and cast parties, you must get to work. *The Tempest* is Shakespeare's last play; it is listed usually among his comedies, and sometimes considered a romance. It does have comedic elements, but touches also on themes of greed, hate, revenge and forgiveness.

As is always the case with Shakespeare, even the smallest of roles is imbued with heart and intellect. The following character notes are meant as a starting point, to help you understand your character. Find what you can here, and then look elsewhere, everywhere, even inside yourself, to find more. Find and use anything, everything, that can help you bring these fun characters to life.

PROSPERO

PROSPERO – Read the Synopsis at the beginning of this book, to be sure you focus on Prospero's back story. His past is what drives him, but Shakespeare began Scene 1 a full twelve years after the actions which formed Prospero's character. Being kicked out of his home, by his own brother, no less! Thrown out to sea, to die! Stranded on a desert island, burdened with the care of his daughter! These are powerful events that are every moment in Prospero's thoughts and memory.

Prospero seems at first content with revenge. He starts out a rather nasty personality, quick to snap at both Miranda and Ariel, and quick to enslave Ferdinand and instruct Ariel to torment the others.

Happily, he grows beyond revenge, and works to bring about a happy future for his daughter, for himself, even for his traitorous brother.

Prospero was always the student, more interested in his books than in running his dukedom. Some fault, clearly, lies with him for his brother's takeover, and it's fair to think Prospero recognizes this, at the end.

Those books he studied and loved? At least one of them was a book of magic spells, the sort of darker magic. he may not have been strong enough when his brother booted him out, but in the years since must have studied more. Turning away from such dark power, at the end, is huge; it shows Prospero's willingness to truly rejoin human society.

Note the game of chess in Act 5: Prospero is a game player. He plays with people, and (as in chess) won by capturing the king. His move to bring Ferdinand together with Miranda secures his return to the King's good graces, and the return of his dukedom.

It is easy enough to misjudge this play to be about revenge, when one should see instead that it is about forgiveness. As Prospero says, "The rarer action is in virtue than in vengeance." (Act 5, Scene 1)

By the way, go to YouTube and watch the 2019 version of *The Tempest* done by the Stratford Festival on Film, to see that Prospero may be reinterpreted as a female character. Theatre legend Martha Henry (at age 80!) does an incredible job inhabiting Prospero, in a version of Shakespeare's play true to each word. (The character has been female before, by Vanessa Redgrave at Shakespeare's Globe in 2000, and by Helen Mirren in Julie Taymor's 2010 film.)

Male or female, Prospero is the mover and shaker who creates the plot of this play, and acts even somewhat as its narrator. His final speech to the spirits is equally addressed to us, asking for applause. Some scholars have even suggested that Prospero is Shakespeare himself, showing how a playwright reveals the world around him

SPIRITS – Oh, what fun! Many or few, in the shadows or on stage in full light, your production will need to determine what the spirits look and sound like, and how they act. They are fun-loving and light-hearted, but capable of instantly becoming ferocious and dangerous. These spirits are of the air and water: light, quickly moved, fun and lively, but also capable of bringing storms.

Often with music-playing abilities, the spirits love dancing and singing.

If you play a spirit, bring joy and life to this fun role!

ARIEL – Chief of the spirits, Ariel shows s/he has more heart even than humans. More intellect, too. Ariel is one of Shakespeare's most beloved characters. (Ariel, by the way, may be female or male; Shakespeare didn't specify, and it hardly matters.)

Like the fairy Puck (*Midsummer Night's Dream*), Ariel can appear solid or be invisible; she's mischievous, spritely, quick to caper about. She laughs easily, and cries just as easily, feeling emotions with great empathy. She is strong, and commands the spirits to do her bidding, so there is very little she couldn't accomplish.

All she truly desires seems to be freedom. However, one can also interpret this play to see her compassion, even love, for Prospero. One could also interpret Ariel to be in control throughout, manipulating Prospero, even changing Prospero to make him more forgiving of his enemies, all to get Prospero to release her.

As powerful and intelligent as Ariel is, Prospero's hold on her is a mystery. After releasing her from the tree-prison, Prospero was somehow able to bind Ariel to his service. Perhaps it's as simple as Ariel living up to her promise, until released. Or perhaps Prospero's control of Ariel comes from Prospero's magic book. (Maybe both are true.)

MIRANDA – Such sweet innocence, perhaps unrivaled in Shakespeare's plays. Miranda has been well educated, growing up under Prospero's tutelage on the island. She is not stupid – far from it! Miranda is naïve in the true "book worm" fashion of someone who has had no practical experience with the world at all.

Note that Caliban's attempted rape has not scarred her psychologically. Her education clearly included the subject of sex, and she understands well what Caliban had in mind. So, too, she recognizes her plight, stuck on an island where there is only one available man (Caliban). The thought of someday bearing children with Caliban is a thought she has accepted, out of necessity – repulsive as she finds Caliban. This is why she jumps so happily when another man (Ferdinand) appears.

It's worth noting that Miranda's naivete may be simply a sign of her young age. Prospero say she was about 3 when kicked out of Milan, which means she is only about 15 now.

Where Prospero is forceful, Miranda is passive, meek, and emotionally vulnerable. But don't think of her as a pushover. She rebukes Caliban; she proposes marriage to Ferdinand; she invites all the men in at the end. Miranda is a mover and shaker like Prospero, in the making.

FERDINAND

Miranda's naivete is easy to excuse, so what about Ferdinand's? He is seemingly just as clueless, and perhaps that means he is also very young; his age is never set out.

Or maybe he's a bit of a simpleton. Just because daddy is king, doesn't mean the boy is bright.

Or perhaps we could choose to see this as an example of what happens when an elite person, like a prince, is educated in an ivory tower, far from "real world" people and concerns. Ferdinand seems intelligent, at times, and at other times seems to parrot a mishmash of words just to get along. He says what is on his mind, perhaps even before thinking it out.

He clearly has a huge heart – his saving grace. He loves his father, and mourns the king's loss deeply. And then falls deeply in love with Miranda. A sharper person may be suspected of simply playing the game: accepting Miranda's love to survive and succeed on the island. Ferdinand's simple and honest nature is important, in that it implies future happiness for the couple. If he was played with a darker side, the ending would be a much different thing.

CALIBAN – Monster to some, Caliban may be pitied. He has known no other home but the magical island, and only dimly remembers his mother. Most of his life has been as Prospero's servant / slave, tortured by Prospero's spirits. He is sometimes portrayed nastily, but other times with more heart.

Prospero notes (Act 1, Scene 2) that his treatment of Caliban grew harsh, only after Caliban tried to rape Miranda. You can interpret such attempted rape as an indication of Caliban's villainy, or perhaps see it as Caliban's own struggles growing up through puberty (his age is never mentioned) with a beautiful girl nearby – the only girl on the island. This exchange also supports the idea that Caliban was nicer at one time, and has gotten nasty as a result of his constant punishments.

Caliban knows the capabilities of the island's spirits more than anyone, as their frequent target. Yet, he apparently experiences only the ugliness and not the beauty.

Though primarily serving as comic relief (with the real clowns, Trinculo and Stephano), Caliban is not stupid or dense. Like Miranda's naivete, Caliban's ignorance comes from growing up knowing nothing else. He is sensitive, and easily hurt, making him a sympathetic villain.

Being of and from the island, one can think of Caliban as an earthy spirit, in stark contrast to Ariel and the rest of his airy spirits. In contrast, Caliban is dark, twisted, harsh, ugly. His speech is full of references to the earth. He lives "below."

Little is clarified of his mother, the witch Sycorax, except that she controlled the island before Prospero arrived. Caliban can be seen as an extension of her earthy powers. He is described as half-man, half-fish; a monster. There is some old power at work in him.

In the end, he renounces following Stephano, and says that he will embrace wisdom. It's at least a hint of turning, and perhaps can be interpreted as forgiveness between he and Prospero.

True comic relief is provided by TRINCULO and STEPHANO – There is an absurd quality to each. Drunkards, and of a lower uneducated caste, yet not stupid – these are, after all, servants to a king.

Trinculo is a sweet follower, easily hurt and offended. Stephano's desire for leadership lays dormant, until he's drunk. (And of course, we see him drunk throughout the play.)

Despite the plot to kill Prospero, these two are lovable and harmless. They are true crowd pleasers, and the more interaction developed between the two of them, the better.

KING ALONSO – Rarely just "Alonso" in this version, to emphasize that there is a king present.

His sorrow at losing his son paralyzes him. On the island, but for a brief moment of rallying his troops to look for Ferdinand, he hardly seems "kingly" and it's easy to imagine Sebastian and Antonio succeeding in their assassination plans.

In productions where Prospero is female, there is an added possibility of relationship between these two. They seem to fit nicely, and such reading adds another level of happy ending.

SEBASTIAN – Easily seen as a villain for attempting to kill his brother, Sebastian is also the very noble, very loyal brother to his King. He does not easily agree to Antonio's scheming, and initially draws his sword to defend the King.

Sebastian is part comic relief. Not a true clown, but part of the comedy. Just how much he deserves to be punished depends upon how he is played, and to what degree he commits to the assassination plot.

ANTONIO – Here is the true villain of the play, although even Antonio receives Prospero's forgiveness

at the end. Antonio took over Milan from Prospero twelve years earlier, and feels no repentance at all. He even tries to double down, by assassinating King Alonso and becoming (King) Sebastian's right hand. While Prospero learns that forgiveness is better than vengeance, one still hopes that Antonio was booted down significantly after Prospero regained his dukedom.

Yet, like all good villains, Antonio is somewhat sympathetic, too. By Prospero's own admission, Prospero was not a good ruler; he was not attentive, and let Antonio do the governing. Perhaps Antonio had the best interest of his people in mind when he took over control.

Antonio is sharp-witted, very intelligent. He is used to manipulating people from behind the scenes.

As Prospero's character arc goes from nasty revenge to loving forgiveness, Antonio's final lines can be interpreted to show he likewise changes. Then again, maybe he remains a villain, and just knows when to say the right thing.

GONZALO – Once in Prospero's employ, when Prospero was the Duke of Milan, Gonzalo is now a trusted advisor to the King of Naples. He is a learned man, who worked his way to the top. While the king and his brother Sebastian were complicit with Antonio's scheme to unseat Prospero, it can be assumed that Gonzalo was not, since he helped save the lives of

Prospero and Miranda. Or perhaps he was in on it, but suffered too much guilt to let them die. In either event, Prospero considers him a friend.

He might be played as a little senile. He is wordy, and somewhat dense; however, the sense of him being so comes primarily from Antonio and Sebastian making fun of him. Gonzalo is erudite and scholarly. He focuses on details (green grass, dry clothes) as a scientist might.

Note, though, that it is he who tries to snap Alonso out of his megrims, and who does a better job leading than any of the others. He can be seen as naïve (thinking his words of comfort would stop the King from mourning his son), but Gonzalo also provides a shining example that kindness and understanding prevails over cunning machinations and plotting.

CAPTAIN – also referred to as the ship's Master.

The Captain is a "hands off" type, letting his First Mate run the ship. Perhaps this Captain is more political appointee, chosen as figurehead to run the King's ship, than true mariner.

FIRST MATE – also referred to as the ship's

Boatswain (pronounced "bo sun"). This is a salty character, one who takes action.

Set Design Notes

The Tempest is perhaps the most easily of all Shakespeare's plays to be done on a minimalistic set, and indeed in Shakespeare's time of traveling actors, often there would have been no set at all.

What set you can build may depend upon what you have. Your space. Your budget. Your available materials. Your time. Your skill level. Your ready help. It's always best to start by recognizing what you have already.

The set for *The Tempest* can be big or small, but it must meet certain needs. Let's list those first, so that sets can be designed first for purpose and second for art:

- <u>The ship's deck and rigging</u>. Staging of the tempest is tricky. It can be as simple as bringing actors forward and creating wild lighting effects behind them. Or construct a partial ship, for the spirits to surround and rock, and from which principal actors can leap.

- Act 1 Scene 2

- <u>"Above"</u>. In the Prologue, and elsewhere Prospero and/or Ariel are "above", which is designed to show their mastery over the stage and its characters. This can be an elevated platform, or scaffolding, or theatre balcony, or perhaps even images projected up onto a scrim, curtain or wall. If not practical, the idea of "above" is not necessary, and these scenes can be played at stage level.

  - Prologue

- <u>In front of Prospero's home</u>. Most of the play is here, at Prospero's door to his cell (home). Indeed, all of Acts 4 and 5. This is a clearing, with an entrance behind or to the side for Prospero's house. Prospero and Miranda have created this island home, from what little they had on their exile boat, so it should be rather crude. Then again, Prospero has grown in his abilities to use magic, so his house can be imposing and magical, too.

  - Act 1 Scene 2
  - Act 3, Scene 1
  - Act 4
  - Act 5

- Epilogue
- special note: chess game (Act 5). Prospero reveals Miranda and Ferdinand playing chess. The symbolism is thick, in that the point of chess is to capture the king, which Prospero has done. Getting Ferdinand and Miranda married is his "checkmate" move, assuring that King Alonso will reinstate his dukedom. A small moment, but one worth consideration.

- <u>Another part of the island</u>. Side spaces, open for movement.

  - Act 2 Scene 1 – where Ariel leaves King Alonso and his men
  - Act 2 Scene 2 – where Caliban gets wood
  - Act 3 Scene 2 – seashore where Stephano landed, and where he hid the liquor
  - Act 3 Scene 3 – where Ariel appears as a harpy to frighten King Alonso

Production License

Shakespeare's play is in the public domain, but this version of it has been created by Brent Nautic Von Horn, who holds all copyright and all rights to performance. (Though, of course, no rights are claimed to Shakespeare's characters and words.)

All rights to perform *Doable Tempest's* version of *The Tempest* on stage for a live audience will be granted to you, almost free of charge, provided:

1. you request a license to use this work from the author at the following email address:

    nauticproductions@yahoo.com

2. you (or your production) purchase at

least ten (10) or more copies of the paperback version of this book *Doable Tempest* from the author (you'll need at least 10 copies of the script for your actors)

3. you send at least 3 pictures of your production to the author's email address above; <u>and</u>

4. that you give credit to the author (Brent Nautic Von Horn) and the book *Doable Tempest* in some nice manner (preferably in your play's program, though on your poster or even in sky writing would be real nice, too)

ALL OTHER RIGHTS are expressly retained by the author, including (without limitation) all rights to film, record, broadcast, stream, or present this work in any manner other than a live performance as above.

www.ingramcontent.com/pod-product-compliance
Lightning Source LLC
Chambersburg PA
CBHW061330040426
42444CB00011B/2842